WOLFE TONE
AND THE COMMON NAME
OF IRISHMAN

HUBERT BUTLER

WOLFE TONE
AND THE COMMON NAME
OF IRISHMAN

THE LILLIPUT PRESS

British Library Cataloguing in Publication Data

Butler, Hubert
    Wolfe Tone and 'the common name of
    Irishman.' — (Lilliput pamphlet series; no. 5)
    1. Nationalism — Ireland — History
    I. Title
    820.5'4'09415   DA938

First published 1985. Design by Jarlath Hayes.
Photoset in 11/12 Baskerville and printed by
Blackrock Printers Ltd., Blackrock, Co. Dublin,
for The Lilliput Press Ltd, Gigginstown,
Mullingar, Co. Westmeath, Ireland.

ISBN 0 946640 09 2

To Dick & Julia

INTRODUCTION

This talk was given in the Mansion House in Dublin on 24 September 1963, the bicentenary of Wolfe Tone's birth.

Much has altered since then, but I believe that my argument has not been affected by the passage of time and that it is pointless to restate it in the terms of 1985 rather than those of 1963.

Yet in the meantime certain things have happened that cannot be ignored. The New Ireland Forum made a valiant attempt peacefully to revive 'the Common Name of Irishman' and to arrest the spiralling violence, which threatens to overwhelm us all, north and south, from which without help we shall never recover. And our history tells us that outside helpers usually come to stay.

The Forum failed of its effect but left a lingering sweetness in the air. The desire for unity and harmony is something like the desire for sleep. Sleep is chased away by too eager a pursuit. It slips in unbidden and unobserved when its time has come, the scarcely valued by-product of some more significant harmony, whose source is elsewhere. 'A healty nation', wrote Bernard Shaw, 'is as unconscious of its nationality as a healty man is of his bones.'

The authors of the Forum Report believe that in the New Ireland 'the cultural and linguistic diversity of the north and south' could be 'a source of enrichment and vitality' and they believe it could be politically guaranteed. Yet how can a government guarantee anything so elusive as the cross-fertilization of cultures? It happens spontaneously or not at all.

Cultural diversity was honoured more than now in the days of Douglas Hyde and his Gaelic League, of Yeats and his colleagues of the Abbey Theatre. They received no government support nor encouragement but they proved that the blending of English and Irish temperaments and talent can be a rich and fruitful one.

The Irish with the defeat and flight of their ruling classes became a peasant people ashamed of their native language, which they associated with subjection and poverty. It was the nineteenth century scholars and writers, mainly men of Anglo-Irish stock, who first gave it dignity and honour. If unity in diversity is ever again to be achieved, it must be done not by governments but by individuals of both English and Irish loyalties. And, in fact, unperceived there is already a slow but steady move in that direction.

There have been 'pairings' of towns and villages in the six counties and and the twenty-six. Unrecorded by the press there have been many cultural exchanges, theatrical, literary or merely social. In this neighbourhood for example the Northern Ireland Project was started in the Christian Brothers School in Carrick-on-Suir. Accompanied by pupils from Kilkenny College, a Protestant foundation, its students visited Ballymena Academy in their Easter holidays and their visit was returned. This has happened for five years now.

Multiply these enterprises by a hundred or a thousand and wait for ten or twenty years, and the dreams of the New Ireland Forum will for the most part be realised. Will there be a United Ireland? Who knows? But the Common Name of Irishmen will have abolished the memory of past dissensions.

Maidenhall,
Bennettsbridge,
Co. Kilkenny.
July 1985.

THEOBALD WOLFE TONE
1763-1798

I regretted, when it was too late, the rather foolish title I have chosen for this talk, 'The Ideology of Tone', for, of course, what made Tone great was that he had no ideology. It was he who first used the famous phrase, 'The Common Name of Irishman', a name with which he hoped to supersede all the ideologies with which the Ireland of his day was divided. Well-known as they are, I shan't apologise for repeating his exact words; it was his ambition, he wrote, 'to unite the whole people of Ireland, to abolish the memory of all past dissensions and to substitute the common name of Irishman in place of the denominations of Protestant, Catholic and Dissenter'.

These talks are supposed to be about Tone's relevance to modern Ireland. Is he a completely out-of-date figure or do his ideas still have something to say to us? And what I want in particular to discuss is this notion of a 'common name of Irishman'. For Tone it was full of gun powder. He expected to overthrow with it the Irish Parliament, to break the connection with England and, with the aid of revolutionary France, to establish an independent Irish Republic. Well, the *explosion* did happen, and appalling havoc was wrought and, though it appeared to many of his contemporaries that all the wrong things were blown up and Irish freedom postponed for some generations and then mutilated, plainly there was dynamism in the idea of 'The Common Name of Irishman'. At least about *that* Tone had not been deceived. Like a great inventor, who blows up himself and his friends with the thing he invents, he had discovered something, which nobody had observed before. He was the father of Irish Republicanism and also I think of Irish nationalism, and since such ideas are very contagious, he was probably answerable in some indirect way for Garibaldi and Kossuth and a dozen national heroes who handled, after him and more effectually, the same explosive material. In most cases their problems were easier than his, for Ireland was more deeply divided than any other country in Europe. Garibaldi and the others wanted to bring freedom to some oppressed but more or less homogeneous and like-minded people, Italian, Polish, Hungarian, Czech. Tone had to invent a nation out of a native majority and a powerful minority which had strong loyalties and affinities outside Ireland. The two parts were linked together by little but a common history and the encircling sea. Even now many people are more impressed by the disaster that befell the United Irishmen than by Tone's discovery that such hostile groups could ever unite under a common name.

In unity they had slowly come to the decision that the Irish government was the worst of all possible governments and that the English and Protestant domination, which it represented, must be overthrown. Tone, a Protestant himself of English descent, decided that this could not be achieved without violence and the help of revolutionary France.

Tone's rebellion, as we know, was an utter calamity and ushered in one of the worst of Irish centuries. The Irish Parliament, corrupt and unrepresentative but at least Irish, was dissolved; the Orange Order, seeing no tyranny but Popish tyranny, swept away the last traces of that Protestant Republicanism of the north on which Tone had based his hopes of a United Ireland. The Catholic Church in Ireland became increasingly segregationist and it was considered godless for a Catholic Irishman to be educated alongside his Protestant compatriots. The Irish people, whose distinctive character the eighteenth century had taken for granted, lost its language and, after the Famine, many of its traditions. A period of industrial expansion was followed by one of poverty and emigration. Finally, the partition of Ireland in the twenties of our century set an official seal on all the historical divisions of our country, racial and cultural and religious, which Tone had striven to abolish.

You might think that all this would have utterly discredited Tone's attempt to link us all together under a common name. Yet it has had no such result, though no one since him has ever achieved even his small success in uniting us.

What dynamism is still left in this old idea of nationalism, and in particular of Irish nationalism? Is it just a faded bit of sentimentality left over from the past, something concerned with shamrocks and Patrick's Day processions and seasonal conviviality? Or has it still the power which Tone discovered in it to supersede a dozen different loyalties, political, racial, material, spiritual, and to unite people who are otherwise disunited in many of their most intimate beliefs?

Is it possible for such an idea to survive into the space age, and, if it has lost all its vigour, should we try to revive it and if so how?

To Tone, of course, as to Grattan and all their contemporaries, Ireland meant the whole of Ireland, north and south, and the dissensions they hoped to abolish had no geographical frontier. The Common Name of Irishman would have been meaningless to them if applied to the twenty-six counties only.

There is another factor that was very important. In Tone's day the majority of Irishmen still lived in Ireland, while today by far the most of the Irish people live outside our island. Two centuries ago, when Tone was born, the idea of a widespread Irish race was not a very significant one, and there was no tincture of *racialism* in Tone's idea of an independent Irish nation. When he was in Philadelphia intriguing with the representatives of revolutionary France about Irish independence, he met many Irish settlers, but though he felt warmly towards them, he did not consider that they had much bearing on the problems of Ireland. *Effective* Irishmen lived in Ireland, which was the Irish nation, and the sentimental ties, which now bind the foreign emigrant to his motherland, were then very weak. That is to say racialism, which in Europe has often since usurped the place of nationalism, hardly existed.

Tone's remarks about the American Irish in Pennsylvania, as about all the European immigrants there, are caustic. He had the view that oppression degrades men and he tended, as did most of the revolutionaries of his time, to look for leadership among those who had escaped it. Of the Pennsylvania Irish, he had a low opinion: after denouncing the ignorant boorishness of the Germans and the uncouthness of the Quakers, he wrote,

> of all the people I have met here the Irish are incontestably the most offensive. If you meet a confirmed blackguard you may be sure he is Irish; you will, of course, observe I speak of the lower orders. As they have ten times more animal spirits than the Germans and Quakers they are much more actively troublesome. After all I do not wonder at it, nor am I angry with them. They are corrupted by their own ignorant government at home and, when they land here and are treated like human creatures, fed and clothed and paid for their labour and no longer flying from the sight of any fellow who is able

to purchase a velvet collar to his coat, I do not wonder if the heads of the unfortunate devils are turned with such an unexpected change in their fortunes and if their new gotten liberty breaks out as it too often does into pettiness and insolence. For all this it is perhaps not fair to blame them.

So when we examine Tone's Common Name of Irishman to see whether it still has validity and power we have to recognise that it concerns our country and not our blood. For him the English or Scots, whose ancestors had settled in Ireland and who made Ireland rather than England the focus of their loyalities and the centre of their interests, became Irish. An Irishman, who went to England or America and acted analogously, became English or American.

I think this rather obvious and platitudinous point is worth stressing because 'nationalism' as a whole has fallen into some disrepute in our centuries. It is regarded, by liberal Englishmen for example, as a sort of petty obstruction in the way of some great brotherhood of mankind, a clot in the bloodstream of universal concord that is to encircle the earth. But if you discuss the matter with them, you will find that they are still obsessed and horrified with the racialist fantasies of the Fascists and Nazis thirty years ago. In fact what they call German nationalism and Italian nationalism were the antithesis of the nationalism of Wolfe Tone. So called Italian and German nationalists of thirty years ago were racialist and anti-nationalists. Hundreds and thousands of men, who lived for centuries under the same hills, beside the same lakes, were all at once told that they were aliens. In their thousands, Germans were ejected from the Tyrol and Slavs from northern Italy. What had this to do with nationalism, which is comprehensive and based on neighbourliness and shared experiences and a common devotion to the land in which you live? It has nothing to do with racial origins. Tone, the father of Irish nationalism, was of English descent and it is absurd that there should ever be any doubts on this matter.

But if you look into the matter more closely you will see how this delusion that racialism was nationalism came about and how it found a very fertile soil in our complicated scientific age, though it is really a very primitive idea. Speed of communications and the growth of world-wide enterprises have made it possible now for people to live in one country and have major loyalities outside it. All over Europe and in Ireland too there are pockets of foreigners, who do not need or wish to be assimilated. You've all read, I am sure, of those vegetable diseases which used to die on the long sea voyage across the Atlantic, but now after a swift and comfortable air-flight arrive in full vigour and ready to ravage a whole continent. It is the same I think with 'the memory of past dissensions', to use Tone's phrase. Our prejudices arrive intact wherever they are exported and it is not as easy as it used to be to eradicate them. We can keep in touch with like-minded people by post in disregard of the person next door; we can get all the support we want for our views by turning a knob on the radio. That is why nationalism, as Tone conceived it, that is to say a concentration of affection for the land in which you live and the people with whom you share it, has become in our day a delicate and fragile plant. It implies an intercourse with your neighbours which is direct and personal, whereas nowadays we need not bother with our neighbours, particularly if, as most people do, we live in cities; there are a dozen impersonal, indirect ways of bypassing our neighbours and being adherents of some remote community.

I remember reading how under Mussolini, Italian school children in Boston used to send their exam papers to be corrected in Italy. But obviously we Irish have been immune from the worst excesses of racialism which we have seen in Europe. And for this surely Tone and those many Irish nationalists of mixed descent and no racial prejudices must have much of the credit. Yet today nationalism is everywhere, sick and discredited. And in the north of Ireland, which was once the seed-bed of republican ideas, the province from which most of the leaders of the United Irishmen derived and from which Tone hoped for the most vigorous support for his movement for national unity and independence, in the north nationalism is very sick indeed. The question is can it be revived and should it be revived? And if so, from what direction will revival come?

Before I discuss this, it occurs to me that I have misinterpreted Tone a little and talked of the Common Name of Irishman as though this was to him an end and not a means. In fact he thought of it as a weapon by which, in his words, 'to subvert the tyranny of our execrable government and to break the connection with England, the never-failing source of all our political evils'.

None of this has much relevance today. If the idea of belonging to a small united nation did recover some of the dignity and power that it had for Tone and his contemporaries, that is not how it could be used. Possibly the connection with England is still an evil in that it is draining away our population and our energy and perhaps implicating us in quarrels and enterprises that should not concern us, but for this England is not to blame, since every year our immigrants leave Ireland for England in huge numbers of their own accord. Many join her army, and fighting against England or the north we should be fighting against our own people with a bitterly divided mind.

In fact, of course, in our very complex and impersonal spaceworld, our enemies are not people or races any longer but ideas and moods and attitudes of mind, and persuasion and understanding are the only effective weapons against these things. The English are not our enemies nor the Russians nor the Chinese. If we think in the military terms, which were valid for Tone, we get into a hopeless impasse. We would not wish to weaken English democracy against Russian Communism. We would not wish to weaken the Russian Communists against the more intransigent and numerous Chinese. Behind every spectre we see a worse one looming from which the first spectre appears to be protecting us, so we had better not see spectres at all but concentrate on the real world, small, personal and concrete, into which we were born. And in this particular sphere the weapon, The Common Name of Irishman, which Tone forged so successfully and used so unsuccessfully, may still have the same power which it always had.

But how are we to re-forge it and against what are we to use it? We have a feeling that everything is wrong but at any moment it is easy to present ourselves with a pleasant and reassuring picture of all being well. In Tone's time it was far easier to diagnose what was wrong for there were extremes of poverty and wealth and glaring injustice. But in his time too one cannot forget that there were plenty of people to paint rosy pictures and to point to the expanding trade, the growing wealth of the country under Grattan's Parliament, and to argue that it was best to leave things as they were. Perhaps it would have been, but we can only stand still in a society where there are no Tones, no men with quick sympathies and passionate convictions and the power to see below the surface. Such a society would perhaps be a

14

tranquil one, but it would be a dead one and Ireland in the 1790s, unlike Ireland today, was very much alive.

A visitor from the 1790s to Ireland today would, of course, be favourably impressed by many things he saw. Three-quarters of the things that Tone fought for have already been achieved and seemingly not by the romantic radicalism, which he espoused, but by the slow and irresistible permeation of liberal ideas, by science, enlightenment, commerce and good communications. Wealth is more evenly distributed, and the religious and political and social discriminations about which we complain in the north and in the south, would seem to this visitor very trifling. Most of them lack legal sanction and are best described in terms of prejudice or ignorance rather than persecution. Look out of any town window and you will see hundreds of television masts, arguing not only growing prosperity but also broadening horizons, a wider knowledge of the world and its problems, a more educated and contented people. What have we to grumble about?

This visitor, if he were Wolfe Tone himself, would probably look for some spirit of revolt seething below the calm surface, but he would fail to find it. In the 1790s Ireland had been in turmoil. Belfast and the north surged with excitement and hope, delighted with the American Revolution and still watching the progress of the French Revolution with passionate interest; in the south there was a great deal of dull and inarticulate misery but among the Protestants there was still the exhilarating memory of the Convention of Dungannon and, with the foundation of the Volunteer Movement, the assertion of Irish Independence. In the Irish Parliament violently opposing views were expressed with eloquence and force. It was a very corrupt and unjust society, but not at all a dead one.

In the 1960s political excitement is subdued, our hopes moderate and, though we are often dull, we can usually articulate our grievances or else escape them. We can go on strike or write a book — and, if all else fails, we can emigrate. It is natural enough that we should be rather low-geared in the expression of our hopes and convictions. Europe has had a whole generation of visions and visionaries. They seem mostly to have ended badly. We have become everywhere, not only in Ireland, very sceptical and we value the man most who has few feelings and no ideas or convictions that are not shared by the passive majority. In fact Ireland today and all Europe is a paradise for the bureaucrat and the Laodicean.

Tone was neither of these and he would have been in no way reassured by the absence of violent discord, the appearance of prosperity. He would have noticed our huge and constant emigration and deduced from it some deep discontent, for how can a man express his dissatisfaction with his country and his despair for its future more emphatically and finally than by leaving it? He would have seen that in 150 years Ireland had become immensely unimportant, unimportant even to herself, and he would probably have argued as before that this was due to her connection with England, which the Act of Union had made more complete. And certainly he would have been staggered by the alteration in their relationship. When he died, Ireland had been in some sort of parity with England, that it to say its population was about half that of England, and Dublin was the second city in the empire. Tone's rebellion was not, like the 1916 rebellion, a wild gesture of defiance, without hope of success. It really might have succeeded. Holland, as Lecky explained, had been no larger when she defied Louis XIV, nor had Prussia when Frederick the Great had turned her into a great power, nor had the United States when she flung off the English yoke. In addition there were far more men of exceptional ability in Ireland than in Holland or Prussia or even the American Colonies. The Protestant gentry had in the Volunteer Movement shown their independent spirit, while the revolutionary doctrines had spread through the industrial north and the Irish Republic would have met with warm support in France and the United States.

I don't think Tone would have been particularly dazzled by the various scientific improvements on which we pride ourselves. He would have observed that, despite them, our society was not the vigorous creative polemical one for which he had worked but stagnant and shrinking. I think he would have noticed in the republic what an Irish priest from Donegal recently called 'the gathering lethargy in rural Ireland'. Father McDyer has more intimate knowledge than most of us, so he will forgive me quoting him. He found that apathy and despair had decimated the population and left ruined homesteads behind it.

Many of the fires that are still sending up smoke are only tended by the enfeebled hands of an aged couple, whose children have gone elsewhere.... What an eloquent commentary [he went on] this was on our age and times. What pillage, persecution and the battering ram failed to achieve, the lure of far-away urban life and the lack of initiative, co-operation and patriotism at home were fast accomplishing.

He had seen thousands of good acres going to loss and he prophesied, 'If we stood by and watched the people flee the land and their houses one after another falling into ruin, all Ireland's struggles will be in vain and the friendly lovable populous Ireland which has existed for centuries would cease to be.'

I repeat this melancholy forecast, because Father McDyer is obviously not a melancholy person; these calamities have acted on him as a challenge. I only wish some Irishman of English descent would face as candidly the far more sensational decay of the other part of the Irish people, Wolfe Tone's people, the Anglo-Irish, and would have as wise and astringent advice to give them. Perhaps he could tell them how they could block their ears to the song of the same siren that has depopulated the West. For of course it is 'the lure of far-away urban life', sometimes called 'broader horizons', that has emptied all the houses where once great decisions about Ireland were made, bold ideas canvassed and the first rough outlines of a great civilisation, half English, half Gaelic but wholly Irish, planned.

Tone was a generous-minded man and I don't think that if he returned to Ireland today he would be at all elated by the complete accuracy with which his sad predictions had been fulfilled. In the last year of his life, when he was aware that the allies upon whom he had counted to make the revolution bloodless had fallen away and that the rebellion on which he was embarking would be hideous and the chances of success very small, he prophesied that his people, the Anglo-Irish of the ascendancy, would disappear, because, he said, they refused to identify themselves with their neighbours, to accept, in fact, 'The Common Name of Irishman'. They have 'disdained', he said, 'to occupy the station they might have held among the People, and which the People would have been glad to see them fill. They see Ireland only in their rent rolls, their places, their patronage,

17

their pensions. They shall perish like their own dung. Those who have seen them shall say, "Where are they?"'

This was an astonishing prediction to have made in 1798 about so numerous, wealthy and powerful and also enlightened a body as the Anglo-Irish ascendancy, but if he returned today he would find it three-quarters fulfilled.

It is the disunity of our country, of course, that is responsible, in part at least, for the stagnation and emigration which one can observe north and south. It has disturbed that equilibrium of opposing forces which is necessary to a country's happiness. Without the Protestant north we have become lop-sided. We lack that vigorous and rebellious northern element, which in the eighteenth century was responsible both for our nationalism and our republicanism. And without the south the north has become smug and has succumbed to what ought to be the most discredited of all contemporary delusions, the lure of broad horizons and all the rest of it.

But let us consider, anyway, the reasons why the north holds aloof. The most important of them is what I've just called Broad Horizons, that is to say the fear of leaving a large world-wide community and becoming attached to a small and insignificant one. The other reasons are all subordinate to this one but I'd better mention a couple of them, both well-known.

The northerners fear that the principles of religious freedom for which their ancestors have fought will be jeopardised under an authoritarian Church.

They speak of loyalty to Britain and its monarchy and to the Anglo-Saxon culture with its great literature and traditions.

Now there is real substance in number two and number three, particularly number two, the authoritarian Church. When Ireland was still united we wrangled about these two things, and, when she is reunited, we shall continue to do so. I'll try to show later that our disputes about these matters, which are sterile in a divided Ireland, would become fruitful in a united one. But I don't believe that at present these disputes are the real source of division.

It is a matter of Broad Horizons and, since we are almost as much hypnotised by them as the Ulstermen are, that is what we have chiefly to consider. All our minds are ranging constantly over the whole world and we are thinking of world-wide opportunities, of international responsibilities, of the exploration of space. The problems of Ireland north and south have begun to seem very puny.

The other day Captain O'Neill, the Premier of Northern Ireland, taking a world view of Ireland in the contemporary manner, said this: 'The prosperity of Ulster largely depends upon the development of the whole British economy and this in turn hangs upon events in the wider world outside. We must always remember that our future may depend as much upon a decision in Geneva or a pay rise in Japan as upon what we decide at Stormont.'

Now what astonishes me about this statement is that it is not expressed as a wail of impotent despair, a lament that the art of government had come to an end and that we are all of us now creatures of almost blind chance. But Captain O'Neill said this with what was obviously a certain proud satisfaction. He and, I suppose, most Ulstermen have adapted themselves to this extraordinary world in which what occurs in Tokyo can be as significant to an Ulsterman as what happens in Limavady or Coleraine. They have come to accept it as something perfectly natural and even rather inflating to their local dignity that they should be linked up so closely with this mighty scheme of affairs, that they are tiny specks on an almost infinite horizon. In the time of Wolfe Tone Belfast was in a constant ferment of intellectual and political excitement. In its ideal it was closer to Philadelphia than to Westminster; it had perhaps a slightly exaggerated view of its importance and some of its admirers even called it the Athens of the North. My point is not that it was at all like Athens but that it wanted to be; today I am sure it does not. The idea of vastness has submerged every national ambition. Ulstermen would be content if the whole of Ireland was the Ballymoney of the Empire or the Cullybackey, the less than Cullybackey of the Universe.

Now this seems to me a disease of the mind, which cannot be treated economically or politically. It seems to me related to the fact that for a century or more Belfast, which once teemed with intellectual vitality, has been sterile and indistinguishable from a thousand other British cities. Not a single new idea has come out of it, whereas Dublin in its most rebellious and discontented period fifty years ago was amazingly prolific in genius.

One can think of a dozen names of European distinction and they all derived from the cross-fertilization of Irish and Anglo-Irish, of Catholic and Protestant culture. In the south, this flowering of genius came to an end when the Anglo-Irish Protestants, who accepted Ireland as their native land, gradually disappeared. It is obvious that the two halves of Ireland need each other and that the Ulster rejection of the south has damaged her as much as it has us.

Yet I do not see how it is any good addressing such arguments to the north while this mood of megalomania, which has affected us too, prevails. It should really, though, be called minimomania, for it means seeing ourselves as a tiny dot on a vast panorama of world events, seeing ourselves unable to communicate with our next door neighbour or influence him except through some great central sorting house, where ideas are collected and redistributed.

While this mood prevails, with us as with them, it's no good offering compromises to the north, by which their religious liberties are guaranteed or their loyalties to the British Monarch or anything else. We have to rediscover first the pattern of the small world and find that our neighbours really are the people next door and not the wage-earners in Japan or some delegates in Geneva. We have to recover some lost arrogance and recognize that we are in fact just as much masters in our own countries as we are masters in our own homes and these remote peoples and conferences need scarcely matter at all. We live in such complex days that it is immensely difficult to prove the obvious. How can one convince Captain O'Neill that the neighbours of the people in Strabane are not the Japanese but the people in Lifford, and that if Newry was on good terms with Dundalk it would not much matter what was thought in Geneva? Perhaps we shall have to be shocked out of these obsessions.

I got a small but helpful shock not long ago. I heard a Belfast man in a pub ask his neighbour, 'Who is Parnell?' He was an intelligent-looking man who probably had a television set and had read all about the Profumo case and knew about the riots in Alabama and about the Buddhist priests who had burnt themselves in Vietnam, but he did not know who Parnell was.

In fact he had such broad horizons, the range of his interests was so wide, that his own place in history had become obscure and unimportant to him. He was befogged and benighted like someone trying to find his way home by a map of the world.

None of this of course would matter if we were with our increased span of knowledge developing a new race of human being, immune from vulgar prejudice and petty jealousy. But in fact we are just as small as we ever were and our minds are just the same size. But some of the best minds are so stuffed with world affairs as to be almost stupefied, immobilized by the great burden of irrelevance that they have to carry round with them. Naturally there is not room for Parnell or indeed for any Irish history, yet the story of Parnell is still supremely relevant to us. All our traditional squabbles about land and property and divorce and morals and non-conformity and democracy, it is all there to be seen and studied in Irish terms and not in Japanese. We cannot afford to cut ourselves off from our history, or from the people and the ideas and the traditions which shaped it, just because we live north of Carlingford Lough. An Irishman *must* know about Parnell, even if it means knowing rather less about Vietnam and Japanese labour conditions.

That is why many are sceptical about our allegedly broadening horizons. When we see a vast forest of television aerials rising over a city we like to think of enlightenment, a deeper understanding of the great world pouring down on us all from the heavens; but does it? Perhaps sometimes it really does. But you can also think of all these masts as ten thousand hypodermic syringes thrust down into our minds to stupefy us and give us the pleasant illusion of participating in remote horrors, with no responsibility for them, and that this enlarged world about which we are always talking is only a sort of drug-addict's hallucination. And that when we wake from it, we shall have lost the power to focus so that we confuse what is real and immediate with what is distant and unimportant. In such a mood we are easily scared by these bogies from Geneva and Japan.

You may think I have put this rather fancifully, so I'll quote to you the same idea, as it was expressed much better than I have done in Wolfe Tone's day by Lord Charlemont. A great Ulster landlord, he never considered Ulster as anything but an integral and vital part of Ireland. And I don't think the problem of reconciling remote loyalties with near ones was ever stated more clearly than he has done.

Let it not be said that Ireland can be served in England. It never was. It is the nature of man to assimilate himself to those with whom he lives. . . . The Irishman in London, long before he has lost his brogue, loses or casts away all Irish ideas, and from the natural wish to obtain the goodwill of those with whom he associates, becomes in effect a partial Englishman, perhaps more partial than the English themselves. . . . Let us love our fellow-subjects as brethren, but let not the younger brother leave his family to riot with his wealthier elder. . .

Where is the English party that is not more or less hostile to the constitutional and commercial interests of Ireland? But Ireland must be served in Ireland. . . . It is the unnatural son who profusely assists in the luxurious maintenance of a beloved alien at the expense of his mother's jointure.

Reasoning like this – and Charlemont was the most reasonable Irishman of his day – we would argue that the Irish Protestant genius in Ulster as in the south was evaporating in the service of England and that to their cost they are neglecting for the maintenance of 'the beloved alien' their duty not only to their Anglo-Irish brothers in the south but their duty to all their Irish compatriots, Protestant and Catholic.

While I'm convinced that this business of Broad Horizons is what is really drawing the north away from us, there are other grounds for dissent, for instance the British Crown and our religious differences. I don't think the disagreement about the Crown is very deep-seated. Catholic scholars who disapprove of nationalism are perfectly correct in tracing the republican and separatist spirit to Protestant origins and in particular to Ulster. Five out of six of the United Irishmen were Protestants. The Protestant gentry, who in 1782 assembled in the church of Dungannon, were fully prepared to make the Duke of Leinster King of Ireland if the royal assent had been refused to their demand for an independent legislature. The American revolt was enthusiastically greeted in the north. There were bonfires in Belfast and riots when dragoons tried to cut down the emblems of Washington. On the other hand the leaders of the Southern Catholics disapproved and sent an address to the king proclaiming 'their abhorrence of the unnatural rebellion' and laying at His Majesty's feet 'two millions of loyal, faithful and affectionate hearts and hands . . . zealous in defence of His Majesty's most sacred person and Government'.

There is scarcely a Protestant in the south, who had not among his forebears a Cromwellian, whose son would gladly have had Charles II decapitated as well as Charles I if any serious effort had been made to restore to the royalists their expropriated lands. And many of them were republicans from principle and not merely from self-interest.

I am saying this not to decry royalism and praise the republic but merely to suggest that north and south there is no ancient and inviolable tradition in favour of one or the other and that to associate the Anglo-Irish with monarchy and the Gaelic-Irish with republicanism is a fantastic misreading of history. If we dropped these hyphens and assumed the common name of Irishman, the question could easily be discussed on its merits.

The religious differences that have divided Ireland are of course more fundamental. Except under Grattan's Parliament and in particular by Tone, little attempt has been made to solve them in the only way they can be solved, that is to say by the Common Name of Irishman. In those days there was a warmth of generosity based on a sudden realization of neighbourliness and a common home. For a short time it succeeded in thawing the rigid frozen barriers of race and creed that divided the Irish. This did not mean any pretence of common blood nor did it mean that doctrinal differences had lessened. Tone was an extreme Protestant, but as secretary of the Catholic Committee he had urgently pressed for full Catholic Emancipation forty years before it was grudgingly conceded. Leaf through his diary and on one page you will find him rejoicing over the calamities that had befallen the Pope through the French Revolution, on the next page he is vigorously defending Catholic liberties against Protestant oppression. He saw the barriers all right but some warm buoyancy of spirit enabled him to leap them.

What is happening today? I can only offer a very superficial and untheological view, but that is the plane on which most of us pass most of our lives so it is perhaps not irrelevant. The Churches are no closer doctrinally than they were in the days of Tone but there is a supposition that new harmony will come from adjustments in dogma and friendly exchanges between ecclesiastics at various conferences in Europe and in America and that this harmony will spread by degrees to distant lands where different religions confront each other, to the frontiers of Catholicism and

Orthodoxy in Central Europe, to the frontiers of Protestantism and Catholicism in Ireland. I hope this is so, of course, and that it is not one of these large-scale ecumenical delusions, but I still think that Tone's way is best. The fact is that difference of dogma has never been a great source of friction in itself and the disappearance of these differences may not bring the brotherhood for which we hope.

Ireland was conquered and anglicised at a time when the English and the Irish shared the same faith. The Orthodox-Catholic friction in Eastern Europe derives not from differences of dogma, which are few, but from the old rivalry between the Austro-Hungarian Empire and Tsarist Russia, between warring cultures in fact. That particular friction still continues and, though it is considered indiscreet to mention this, it has in our day caused immeasurable persecution and slaughter.* On the other hand, as you know, many hundreds of Protestant sects are now at peace with each other without in the least agreeing. They have reached this by conceding to each other the Right of Private Judgment, or, as it could often be called, the Right to be Wrong. This arrangement has worked very well and one of the Founding Fathers of the USA, President Madison, even declared that American Religious Harmony was based on a multiplicity of sects, all of them disagreeing with each other.

The Right of Private Judgment for Irish Catholics, as well as for Irish Protestants, was vigorously sustained by the Volunteers in a proclamation from Dungannon in 1782. It ran:

> That we hold the right of private judgment in matters of religion to be equally sacred in others as ourselves. Therefore that as men, as Irishmen, as Christians and as Protestants we rejoice in the relaxation of the Penal Laws against our Roman Catholic fellow-subjects and that we conceive the measure to be fraught with the happiest consequences to the union and to the prosperity of the people of Ireland.

There was a difficulty of course; it was not clear how the centralized and authoritarian Catholic Church could ever reciprocate by conceding to Protestants the right to be wrong. .Because of this doubt Charlemont, the head of the Volunteers, and Henry Flood, both of them good Irishmen and in no way bigotted,

---

*See *Escape from the Anthill* (Mullingar 1985), pp. 10-12, 270-305.

withdrew their support of full Catholic Emancipation. Their dilemma was surely a real one and it is useless to reproach the Ulstermen with bigotry because fifty years ago they resisted Home Rule on religious ground and because the same objections were repeated at the time of Partition.

We must find some way of living together and I think Tone's way, the way of generous inconsistency, is still the best. After all we all of us respect the two opposing principles of authority and private judgment. Everyone in the world regulates his conduct by both, deferring sometimes to traditional authority, sometimes to his own rebellious sense of fitness, or, as some Protestants say, his Inner Light. The Catholic Church is held by us in Ireland to be the principal guardian of Authority and the Churches of the Reformation are held to be the guardians of Private Judgment. This of course is only a rough approximation to the truth since many of the post-Reformation sects, the Mormons, for example, are authoritarian. But it is reasonable to think that social harmony in a united Ireland would be based on an equilibrium of these two opposing forces, an equilibrium which Partition has disastrously disturbed. Opposition is inevitable, since we are all differently constituted and, if the clash of opposites was muffled or arrested, society would come to a standstill like a clock whose pendulum had ceased to swing. We may even come to be grateful for sharp expressions of opposition and only disturbed when, as in totalitarian countries, dissent is dead and every emphatic 'Yes!' does not meet its equally emphatic 'No!'

If Ulstermen started arguing about these matters again, it would I believe be a hopeful sign. It would mean that they were returning from the world of Broad Horizons, where such disagreements are subordinated to salesmanship, to the small and stable personal world, where we do disagree about important things but the Common Name of Irishman has power to reconcile us. Let me repeat that broad horizons are all right for Standard Oil or for the export of sewing machines, but for the ordinary man, with limited sensibilities and limited intellectual capacities, they are best avoided. In the long run it means the export of men and women who are much more important than oil. A child could see that the reason why Captain O'Neill feels himself to be imprisoned in Stormont by the Japanese is because, for 150 years, we have been exporting all the brains and all the energy through which these not very difficult problems could be solved.

You will probably think my arguments specious and in fact we will possibly not recoil from broad horizons till we have suffered from them ourselves. We make plenty of jokes about the inefficiency of international bureaucracy but we have not yet seen for ourselves its heartless cruelty.

Twenty years ago the French Catholic writer, Francois Mauriac, saw something at a Paris railway terminus which caused him to say that an era had ended. That dream of progress through enlightenment and science, which men had conceived in the eighteenth century, had collapsed for ever.

What he had seen in Paris was a lot of small boys and girls between the ages of two and fifteen crowded into cattle waggons. He did not know at the time that there were over 4000 of them and that they were going to be killed and burnt in Poland. Very few people did really know this for it was one of those vast impersonal bureaucratic enterprises, in which everyone, engine-drivers, policemen, typists, civil-servants, everyone did his duty and delegated responsibility to someone else and no one felt qualified to intervene. Mauriac did not condemn the French or the Germans or their allies, but the whole modern world of centralized and scientific bureaucracy. And surely he was right.

Remember, for example, that in Nazi-controlled Europe the strongest resistance to those deportations, which have made our century the most barbarous in history, came not from the great imperial peoples but from some small ones like the Danes and the Bulgarians. They assumed in others the same attachment to their native land which they felt themselves – and they resisted.

So I don't think that Tone is a backnumber at all, or that his pattern of small-scale loyalties has been superseded by the march of history and the increasing unity of mankind and all the rest. All that is empty newspaper talk. There is nothing sentimental or self-loving about Tone's ideal of 'The Common Name of Irishman', and it still has potential dynamism. If we think anything else, we have misunderstood Tone, a practical, adventurous, much-travelled man, who sentimentalized nothing and nobody and had no very inflated idea of himself or his country or his countrymen. All the dangerous and sentimental dreams nowadays are international, and imperial and oecumenical. It is because of these dreams that we talk about masses and classes, about inferior and superior races, about the white man's burden and the black man's rights, about cosmic clashes between Truth and Error. These dreams have caused extraordinary convulsions and are likely to cause more. Tone had no international or oecumenical ideas at all and though he was a revolutionary and a rebel he did not idealize either the 'toiling masses' or the Irish race. He was simply an Irishman, at a time when the existence of such a phenomenon was widely disputed.

Tone travelled to Europe and America by means of sails and horses yet I think he had just as good an understanding of what men are like as we have, who go by jet. *His* was still a very personal world; there was no such thing as a Public Relations Officer, so the son of the bankrupt coachmaker from Bodenstown interviewed the heads of governments and the generals of armies. He promoted two invasions of Ireland and accompanied them himself. Perhaps he acted foolishly, but at least he acted for himself and took full responsibility for his actions. He was not like some modern conscript warrior, whose enemies are all chosen for him by some distant authority, and who, because of that, expects to be excused for the crimes which he commits, explaining that he did them under orders in association with 20,000 others.

Has this personal world of Tone gone beyond recall? Are we totally committed to the impersonal world in which we do everything through our representatives and nothing by ourselves? Let us anyway be quite clear what sort of society ours is. It is one of which the Paris episode I related is so typical that it has escaped comment. Possibly we don't talk about these things, because men don't talk about maladies which they believe to be incurable. Subconsciously perhaps we think that our world would be better blown up and that is why the great powers are making such strenuous efforts to do so and the small ones are offering such feeble resistance.

But I can't see that the situation is incurable or that the personal world in which we are responsible for our own actions and our neighbour is the man next door has irrevocably gone. Here in Ireland the fabric of this old personal world, though it has been split in half, is still both sides of the border, fairly sound, and I think we could maintain it.

I think we shall extricate ourselves from the world of broad horizons before we are blown up. The disentangling process will of course be very long, but as other nations, as soon as they realize what is happening, will be engaged in it too, it will be a co-operative undertaking.

I ought to end with a quotation from Tone himself, but he was a warm impulsive man who broke into history simply because the reflective men had failed. I don't think there is an opening yet for impulsive men like him and I'd prefer to quote again from Charlemont, the reflective Ulsterman, whom Tone pushed aside.

> Like circles raised in the water by the impulse of a heavy body, our social duties as they expand grow fainter, and lose in efficacy what they gain in extent. . . . The love and service of our country is perhaps the widest circle in which we can hope to display an active benevolence. . . . If every man were to devote his powers to the service of his country, mankind would be universally served.

I don't think this is just a piece of eighteenth-century rhetoric. I am sure it has the universal validity of a geometrical formula. If we assumed the Common Name of Irishman and acted within the narrow circle of our capacities, there would be no need for campaigning or crusading about the border. North and south we would apply ourselves to a thousand urgent problems, social and material and personal, which since the death of Tone we have been taught to regard as parochial and beneath our dignity, and which we have neglected for 150 years. One day we should find that almost without our knowing it the border had gone.